Foreword

Come Holy Spirit comprises the papers and sermons delivered at the Trinity Institute Conference of 1974.

Trinity Institute, as an instrument for continuing education of the clergy of the Episcopal Church, was conceived and developed by the Rev. Dr. Robert E. Terwilliger. The conferences of the Institute have brought to Episcopal clergy — and laypeople — the best theological minds of the world. Distinguished lecturers and preachers have shared contemporary thoughts arising in virtually every branch of Christendom. The benefits accruing to the entire Episcopal Church are incalculable.

Come Holy Spirit is dedicated to the Rt. Rev. Robert E. Terwilliger, Suffragan Bishop of Dallas, in gratitude for his work as Director of Trinity Institute and with a prayer that, as bishop, his ministry will continue to enrich the Church.

The Publishers

Contents

The Eucharistic Sermon

**The Right Reverend and
Right Honourable
Arthur Michael Ramsey
Sometime Archbishop of
Canterbury**

The Cost of Renewal

The Gospel of St. John, chapter 14, verse 16: "I will pray the Father, and he will give you another Comforter."

I greet all of you who have come to share in this Eucharist tonight. Peace be with you. In the following days, we are going to be studying together and praying together about the theme of the Holy Spirit. Much will be said about the gifts of the Holy Spirit. But, first, I want to speak to you, not about the Spirit's gifts, but about the cost of his coming to us and the cost of our renewal by him today. That cost is Calvary.

It was in answer to the prayer of our Lord that the

Father gave the Spirit, and today it is in answer to our own prayer that the gift is renewed. Jesus says, "I will pray the Father, and he will give you another Comforter." But what was the prayer of Jesus that issued in such a stupendous result? Was it just one sentence? Or was it just one movement of the heart? "I will pray the Father . . . ."

That prayer was the total offering of himself to the Father's will and glory. It was a prayer that comprised all Jesus did and all Jesus accepted from the moment he steadfastly set his face toward Jerusalem until the moment his journey to the Father was completed in Heaven. Inwardly, it was a prayer whose depths of love, and agony, and joy our minds cannot grasp. Outwardly, it was a prayer disclosed to sight and hearing in some of the scenes of the Passion.

"I will pray the Father . . . ." Before Jesus and the Apostles leave the upper room, there is a glimpse of this prayer in St. John 17: "Father, the hour has come; glorify thy Son that the Son may glorify thee . . . . For their sake I consecrate myself, that they also may be consecrated in truth."

Then we pass from the upper room to the garden. And going a little further, he fell on the ground and prayed that if it were possible, the hour might pass from him. And he said, "Abba, Father, all things are possible to thee, remove this cup from me, yet not what I will, but what thou wilt."

We pass on to the hill of Calvary, and there, indeed are prayers of Jesus: his prayer for the forgiveness of his tormentors . . . his prayer for himself in the black dereliction . . . and his prayer for himself, as he entrusts himself in death to the Father's keeping. But the prayers of Jesus were not only the words he uttered. The death itself was a part of "I will pray the Father . . ." and so on right through to the last indescribable stage of the journey to the Father's face. Yes, the prayer of Jesus was that, and the cost of the giving of the Paraclete was that.

Not for a moment do we think of this sacrificial prayer of Jesus as something demanded to cause the Father to be gracious, or to elicit a gift that might otherwise be reluctant to flow out to meet the needs of mankind. No! Christ's offering was one with the divine self-offering, one with the eternal glory of the Father and the Son, the glory of the self-giving love of eternal diety; costly, divine love in the heart of God, issuing in costly love in time and history.

Two scenes portray vividly the self-giving that lay behind the gift of the Paraclete. There is the scene on Calvary described by St. John after Jesus has died. The soldier comes and pierces his side with a spear and from his side there flows water and blood. Why this intense emphasis by the Evangelist upon the water and the blood flowing from the side of the dead Jesus? Because it happened historically and it is history that he is emphasizing so strongly. More than that, knowing St. John and knowing his love of symbolism, we see in the water and the blood the flowing of cleansing and life from Christ crucified. "The Sacraments," wrote E. C. Hoskyns, one of my own great teachers, "are not two

independent rites, but the means whereby each
faithful Christian is enabled to stand on Calvary
with the beloved disciple and receive that purifica-
tion and that new life which is the life of the Spirit."

This theme recurs on the evening of Easter Day.
Jesus appears to the Apostles in the room where
they have locked themselves in in fear, greets them
with his peace, and shows them the wounds in his
hands and his side — the side the spear had
pierced, from which the water and the blood had
flowed. It was as he showed them the wounds that
he breathed on them and said, "Receive the Holy
Spirit." The tremendous gift is here; the prayer of
Jesus is answered.

"I will pray the Father, and he will give
you . . . ." What a prayer it has been. The prayer
has been rooted in divine sacrifice, and no wonder,
for the gift itself is utterly sacrificial. This other
Paraclete is the spirit of the crucified and risen
Jesus. And it is as the spirit of the crucified and
risen Jesus that he is the author of power and joy.

What was true of the Spirit's first coming in the
Apostolic Age is true of spiritual renewal in our own
or any age. *Come thou, Holy Spirit, come.* We
make that prayer and we have that hope under the
shadow of Calvary and under the light of Jesus.

First, then, the renewal of the Church by the
Holy Spirit is inseparable from the Holy Spirit
convicting the Church. He shall convict when he is
come. Our sins as a Church are exposed to him.
And what are those sins? He knows. Perhaps
complacency with our religious and material
prosperity. Perhaps insensitivity to the sufferings of

the many in the world in whom Christ himself suffers. Perhaps, on the other hand, our shallow activism that neglects the discipline of prayer and the discipline of penitence. Or that contemplation of God without which we may starve our own souls and, perhaps, starve the souls of others who are looking to us for spiritual help.

Let the Spirit convict. For only as he convicts, does the Spirit renew. And we pray, "Revive, O Lord, Thy work in the midst of the years, in the midst of the years make it known, in wrath remember mercy."

So too, the Holy Spirit renews the Church by bringing us near to Calvary. After all, the language of death comes so much into our worship, our liturgy, our piety. We say that we were baptized into the Lord's death, and we feed upon the Lord's broken body. But where, men may ask, is the counterpart in our lives? Where does Christ call on us to be ready to suffer, to be ready to suffer in face of the agony of the world's suffering? Or, perhaps, in relation to our own sins, which crucify the Lord afresh? Somehow or other, authentically, near to Calvary and nowhere else, is the renewing power of the Holy Spirit, the message of the water and the blood flowing from the Savior's side.

But, dear Christian people, be of good courage. Renewal by the Holy Spirit is happening. The Holy Spirit is at work. I have, myself, seen enough of Christian life in many countries to be sure that the Holy Spirit is not dead. The Holy Spirit is working mightily, sometimes within what we call the institutional Church, and sometimes on its periphery, or indeed, far beyond it.

In two particular ways the Holy Spirit is working among young people in many countries. One is the passionate concern about human suffering and the desire to serve and help those who suffer. The other is the hunger for prayer and contemplation, the renewal of depth in religion. And sometimes those two streams — the stream of concern for social justice and the stream of prayer and contemplation — are seen flowing together. This is vividly to be seen in the community of Taize. Both streams are of the Holy Spirit, and both flow ultimately from the wounded side of Jesus. It was with the Spirit of the Lord upon him that the Messiah at the synagogue at Nazareth spoke of his mission to the poor, the captives, the mourners, and the downtrodden. And no less it is by the Spirit making intercession within them, with groanings that cannot be uttered, that Christians learn to pray "Abba, Father" and to lift up their souls to their Creator.

Tonight, we face the cost. In this Eucharist, we are once again nearer to the heart of our Lord's words, "I will pray the Father, and he will give you another Paraclete." For here, before the Father and before us, is the memorial of Calvary. The Sacrament is no independent rite, but a means whereby the faithful christian stands on Calvary with the beloved disciple. Yes, we stand with the beloved disciple as the water and the blood flow from the side of Jesus.

Soul of Christ, sanctify me.
Body of Christ, save me.
Blood of Christ, invigorate me.
Water from the side of Christ, wash me.
Passion of Christ, strengthen me.
O, good Jesus, hear me,
Within thy wounds hide me.
From the malicious enemy defend me.
Suffer me not to be separated from thee.
In the hour of my death, call me,
And bid me come to thee.
That with thy saints I may praise thee
Forever, and ever.

With thy saints, praise thee; the Holy Spirit is the *arrabon,* the first fruits of our inheritance. He is the power of the age to come, the spirit of glory. It is he who keeps alive in us the vision of Heaven, that eternal perspective in which our existence day by day is spent. May he, day by day, renew that vision in us.

**The Right Reverend
Arthur Michael Ramsey**

**Sometime Archbishop of
Canterbury**

The Spirit and the Apostolic Age

My role within this seminar is the modest role of a student of theology, and we are going to explore and study together the doctrine of the Holy Spirit, as revealed in Holy Scripture. Today, we shall think of the experience and concept of Holy Spirit in the Apostolic Age. Tomorrow, we will consider, especially, the teaching about the Holy Spirit in the Fourth Gospel, for we may find that the concept of the Spirit of Glory in the Fourth Gospel gathers up explicitly much that is implicit in the other parts of the early Christian tradition.

There are those who find something very elusive about the Holy Spirit in the Bible. And I believe that by facing that elusiveness frankly and not being shocked by it, we are going to find the greatest depths in the doctrine. This elusiveness has been reaffirmed recently by Dr. Richard Hanson in an essay contained in a very valuable book, *The Attractiveness of God.* Dr. Hanson reminds us that in the Old Testament there is no clear concept of the Holy Spirit as a being, and the phrase, "the Spirit of God" is used of the divine activity, like other phrases such as "the hand of the Lord," "the arm of the Lord," and "the word of the Lord." And coming to the New Testament, Dr. Hanson says this: "The doctrine of the Holy Spirit as a separate hypostasis, as a person within the godhead, is inadequately supported in the New Testament."

That sounds rather negative, but Dr. Hanson goes on to say that, while there is little that the New Testament shows us about the Spirit as a phenomenon in himself, it is clear that the role of the Spirit as the Spirit of God is tremendous. "The Holy Spirit is God as he has manifested himself as free and sovereign over even the history of revelation." It is also clear, says Hanson, that the Holy Spirit is God continually bringing the Church into an encounter with the events of the career of Jesus Christ — the incarnation, the crucifixion, the resurrection and the ascension. Elusive in distinctive definition, tremendous in the power of divine and human relationship — such is the Holy Spirit and we may find that with the Holy Spirit, as with Christ himself, it is in this mysterious self-effacement that the overwhelming power and glory shines out.

Let me refer to another book which is, I think, the most valuable and significant recent book about the doctrine of the Holy Spirit. It is entitled *The Go-Between God,* and the author is John V. Taylor. Taylor suggests that relationship between phenomena and especially relationship between person and person is the very nature of God's activity in creation and in salvation. "As a believer in the creative spirit, I would say that deep within the fabric of the Universe, the Spirit is present, as the go-between which confronts each individual phenomenon with the beckoning reality of the larger whole and compels it to relate to others in a particular way." Again, he says, "the creator Spirit works from the inside of the processes but only by startling his creatures into awareness and encounter with one another, prompting them to higher degrees of consciousness and creating the necessity for choice in one situation or another." And then, following this line of thought, Taylor says, "Self-sacrifice is inherent in this divine go-between concept. A principle of life through death, of individual self-immolation in the interests of a larger claim."

From these analogies in the sphere of creation, Taylor goes on to Spirit as the go-between in the inner life of the godhead and the go-between in the relation between God and ourselves, his human creatures. God's Spirit evokes our consciousness of ourselves, as Christians, our awareness of Jesus as Lord and our awareness of the Father to whom we pray, crying, "Abba, Father." And it may, thus, be difficult to speak about holding communion with the Holy Spirit. Why? Because the Spirit is, himself, communion.

From that background, let us have a rapid glance at the Old Testament. In the books of the Old Testament, the English word "spirit" translates two Hebrew words, one of them meaning "breath" and the other meaning "wind," and both Hebrew words speak of the divine activity in the world. Divine breath keeps human beings alive, and thus Elisha prostrates himself on the dead body of the son of the Shunamite woman and breathes into him, and his life revives. So too, the world of nature is kept alive by divine wind. "When thou takest it away they die and return again to their dust, when thou lettest thy wind to go forth, they are made strong, and thou shalt renew the face of the earth." And the phenomena of stupendous and startling strength in human lives are due to divine wind: the strength of a Samson, the ecstacy of the prophets. When this divine wind seizes hold of Saul and Saul goes dancing around with the prophets (they say, "Is Saul also among the prophets?"), it is this divine wind that has uplifted him. Spirit speaks thus of the dependence of the world and mankind upon deity, deity within and beyond.

But there is in the Old Testament the constant looking forward. And one of the things to which the Psalmists and Prophets looked forward was a day when the Holy Spirit would be disclosed in a more significant way than ever before. And this coming disclosure of the Spirit will be in three relationships: to the Messiah, to the community, and to the cosmos. The prophetic writings include not only descriptions of the ideal king endowed with the Spirit's gifts, but of the community's renewal by the Spirit's outpourings and of the world renewal as well. What was not foreseen was the close relation, in the time of fulfillment, between the Messiah and the community who came to share in the Messiah's own anointing. "Look, Father, look on his anointed face, and only look on us as found in him." In due time, the Messiah appears.

The Cardinal has spoken about the lovely mystery of the conception, the response of the blessed Virgin Mary, and the birth. So, let me start at the Lord's baptism. At the time of the Lord's baptism in Jordan the Holy Spirit descended upon him in the sign of the dove and a heavenly voice proclaimed him the unique, or only, Son. Meanwhile, the Baptist had predicted that this greater one, coming after him, would be the author of a baptism, as compared with which John Baptist's own baptism would seem a very small affair.

What was this baptism going to be? In Mark's account, the coming one will baptize in Holy Spirit. In the Matthean-Lucan account, however, there is possibly a double baptism. Jesus is going to baptize in the Holy Spirit and in fire, and we cannot be quite certain what lies behind this imagery. Does it refer to one baptism that is both wind and fire? A prophecy of what happened at Pentecost? Or is it a foretelling of two baptisms — a baptism of fiery judgment upon an impenitent nation, and a baptism of Spirit, of salvation, to those who receive it? I do not think we can be quite sure, but the possibility of this double baptism — a baptism of judgment being one thing, and the baptism of the Spirit being another — is at least suggested by the striking saying, later in St. Luke's Gospel, "I came to cast fire upon the earth and would that it were already kindled. I have a baptism to be baptized with; and how I am constrained until it is accomplished!" But, certainly, this saying does suggest that the mission of Jesus is going to issue in fiery judgment on the nation and in waters of suffering under which he himself must be plunged. It is out of this fiery judgment and out of Christ's own baptism into deep suffering that the great gifts of the new covenant are going to be released.

Each of the Synoptic Gospels describes Jesus as fulfilling his ministry in the power of the Spirit; and Mark, in his account, is not afraid of the age-old physical imagery. The Spirit drove him into the wilderness to be tempted of the Devil. It is in the power of the Spirit that Jesus does his work. According to the synoptists Jesus says very little about the Holy Spirit, either as a present or a future gift. There is the bit of teaching about blasphemy against the Holy Spirit, and that was evoked by the mental darkness of those Pharisees who attributed Jesus beneficent works to an evil power and who drew from him some words about the Holy Spirit. And there was also the teaching about how, when the Apostles in future days were hauled before kings and governors, they need not worry about what to say because the Holy Spirit in that hour would guide them.

Why this reticence about the Holy Spirit? We can guess. One likely reason was that Jesus was, in any case, being reticent about his Messiahship, lest his Messiahship be understood in inadequate and superficial ways. Again, he was reticent about the Spirit because the concept of the Spirit was going, in due time, to be revolutionized by his death and resurrection. If he spoke about it, premature, inadequate, ideas about the Holy Spirit might grow and be perpetuated.

But the go-between concept may provide another reason for this reticence. If Jesus was himself filled and directed with the Holy Spirit, as no one else ever had been, the effect of his being filled by the Spirit was to deepen, not a kind of Spirit-consciousness as an isolated thing, but rather his consciousness of the *Father*. It was the Spirit of the Father communicating deep in his being the Father-Son relationship. Note the significant episode that St. Luke records: "In that hour Jesus rejoiced in the Holy Spirit and said 'I thank thee, Father, Lord of heaven and earth.' " Just because the Holy Spirit is go-between, there is in Jesus' elusive reticence, perhaps a sign of the immense significance of the Holy Spirit as being communion between Father and Son.

We come now to the day of Pentecost. According to Luke's Gospel, Jesus had, in the city of Jerusalem, after the resurrection, told the Apostles to tarry in the city until they were endued with power from on high. On the day of Pentecost, the gift comes to the expectant body of disciples in Jerusalem. On that day violent things were seen and heard: rushing wind, what seemed like tongues of fire resting on each of the disciples, and then, an outburst of praise in other tongues, praising the wonderful works of God. And while St. Luke appears to take the other tongues to mean a miraculous gift of foreign languages, it seems more likely that what happened was an outburst of speaking with tongues, the wordless outbreaking of praise, the *glossolalia,* described elsewhere in the Acts and the Epistles.

But stupendous things are happening, and together the wind and the fire, and the outburst of praise, and the intense fellowship of the company make it clear that something otherworldly had been happening. The bystanders could only suppose that the Christian disciples must be drunk. That allegation gives Peter his opportunity of a lifetime, and he addresses the crowd in Jerusalem: "We are not drunk, but what is happening is the fulfillment of the prophecy of Joel: the outpouring of Holy Spirit in the last day." But follow Peter's speech to near the end, because it is near the end that he says the tremendous revolutionary words. He speaks of how Jesus died, rose again, and was exalted; and this was the death, resurrection, and exaltation of the Messiah as foretold in Scripture. Then he adds these words: "This Jesus, having received from the Father the promise of the Spirit, has poured out this which you see and hear. This Jesus, crucified, exalted, is the author himself of the day's stupendous happening. Jesus is, in the service of the Father and in dependence on the Father, the giver of the Holy Spirit." And that is the great revolution — Holy Spirit is supremely the Spirit of Jesus. And not surprisingly, elsewhere throughout his narrative of the apostolic mission, the writer describes the Spirit frequently as "the Spirit of Jesus." The Spirit of Jesus is mentioned, advising, prompting, urging, forbidding.

Tomorrow we shall see how St. John draws out the inner relation between the Holy Spirit and Christ's death and resurrection and his glory. But just now, let us look at the broad picture of the Church in the Apostolic Age, and see some glimpses of this new revolutionary doctrine of Holy Spirit and how it is operating.

First, the old impersonal imagery continues: wind, fire, and water. Do not quench the Spirit, says St. Paul. Do not make foolish attempts to put out the fire. The old imagery, physical imagery, is there. Yet the language of personality also appears. The Spirit wills, chooses, forbids, prays, intercedes, grieves. "Grieve not the Spirit," says St. Paul, as well as "quench not the Spirit." The Spirit is personal. And while Spirit in the Christians is the self-effacing go-between, bringing them the consciousness of Jesus as Lord and urging them to say Jesus is Lord, and bringing them the awareness of the Father as they pray, "Abba, Father," he is himself no less personal than the Father and Son are personal. Indeed he is called both the Spirit of God and the Spirit of Jesus.

Is it not here that we see the germ of Trinitarian belief in the Church? Trinitarian belief grew not from the speculations of clever men, but from the native soil of Christian experience. We see the beginnings of Christian Trinitarian belief in a phrase like this (Ephesians 2:18): "Through whom [that is through Jesus] we have access in one Spirit to the Father," or the salutation at the end of 2 Corinthians: "The grace of our Lord Jesus Christ and the love of God and the fellowship of the Holy Spirit be with you." Written into the Christian doctrine both of God and of man is what Joseph said to his brethren. "You shall not see my face unless you bring your brother with you." Relationship — human and divine — that is what the doctrine we are studying is really about.

The Holy Spirit teaches fellowship, a new note of unity appears in the experience of the first Christians. The note of unity appears in the experience of Pentecost, where the participants are lifted out of themselves into a common ecstasy of praise. It appears also when we read of their being "of one heart and one soul," and in the sharing of their property in common. But the fellowship of the Holy Spirit had a depth of divine-human relationship, a relationship of go-between that we might easily miss in any superficial thought and language. Let me take one passage where St. Paul strikingly draws out fellowship, not just as a society, but as a quality. I refer to Philippians, chapter two: "If there is any encouragement in Christ, any incentive of love, any participation in the Spirit, any affection and sympathy, complete my joy by being of the same mind, having the same love, being of full accord and of one mind, do nothing from selfishness or conceit, but in humility count others better than yourselves." Each of those phrases tells, and the interlocking of all those phrases tells. But perhaps a key phrase is, "if there is any participation in the Spirit." To share in the Spirit is to be living already outside oneself and in the brethren.

But what is the range of this fellowship? What is it's relation to geography and history, to place and time? To know the answer, we have to glance at some of the other characteristic words describing fellowship in relation to the doctrine of the Spirit.

One description is *"ecclesia."* The Christians united to Christ by faith and baptism are a spiritual race and nation, the new Israel whose unity is basically that of the brotherhood of spiritual race — in Peter's words, an elect race, a holy nation, a priesthood for God's own possession. So that the *ecclesia* in any place, the *ecclesia* in Corinth, the *ecclesia* in Philippi, the *ecclesia* in New York, means the one Christian people as manifested in Corinth, Philippi, or New York — the members of the race who happen to be living there.

Another word is *Soma,* body, and this word speaks more intimately of the union of Christians with Christ and with one another. As the body of Christ, the Christians are the organ of Christ in the world. In one Spirit we were all baptized into one body, and all made to drink of one Spirit. And as participation in the Holy Spirit involves participation in and with one's fellow Christians in union with Christ, so the growing together and growing up of the members of the body means their growing into the fullness of Christ's own life, growing into Christlikeness so that Christ will one day be totally

manifested in those who are his members. And if 1
Corinthians 12 describes the body as it now is with
the many gifts serving its common life, Ephesians 4
tells us vividly of the Christian life as our growing
together into Christ's own holiness, right up to the
fullness of his own manhood.

This Christian fellowship was not a shapeless
fellowship. It had a shape and it has a shape still,
though that shape is theologically speaking, a very
simple and rudimentary one. There is the rite of
Baptism, whereby men and women are initiated
into the Body of Christ; and there is the rite of
Eucharist, whereby they are fed with Christ's own
life as they make memorial of his death. And there
is an apostolic ministry of word and sacrament.
And both sacraments and ministry witness to the
historic continuity of the ecclesia and to its
universality. To say that is to bring us to the verge
of the difficult questions about the relation of Spirit
and institution in Christianity. And indeed, I think
it is in the awareness of those difficult questions
that we have gathered here this week. I will not
pursue that particular question much further this
morning, because two years ago I discussed it
specially in the seminar here in Riverside Church,
and my discourses were published in the book The
Charismatic Christ. But forgive me for repeating
now a few sentences with which I then ventured to
sum up my discussion. "We are called to cherish
the horizontal tradition that reaches across the
centuries and also to be alert to the vertical actions
of the Spirit in the here and now. To do this is a
difficult adventure, and we may fail to find a

logical synthesis of what we are doing. But it is not an adventure that need injure our souls. Our souls would rather be imperiled if we were to be content either to rest within a static structure of tradition or to be swept into some enthusiastic movement of the day without relating it to the larger world of catholic truth and life."

In this connection, just a word about the Sacrament of Holy Baptism and about one or two gifts of the Spirit, which are sometimes strongly emphasized.

It was by baptism, a rite in water, that people were initiated into the Body of Christ, made to drink of one Spirit. "Repent and be baptized," said St. Peter, "and you shall receive the Holy Spirit." When people were baptized, a number of things happened. There is evidence that they said the Lord's Prayer together. There is evidence that they praised God with joy in their hearts, and that is not surprising. There is evidence that sometimes after Baptism there was speaking with tongues. There is evidence of one occasion at Ephesus when the newly baptized both spoke with tongues and prophesied. Yet the term, "Baptism," properly belongs to the one Christian initiation, and that is never to be repeated. Again and again, in the life of the Church, there are renewals of the Holy Spirit, and those renewals may be of exciting kinds, recapturing the meaning of Christian vocation. But to call such experiences Baptism is, I believe, very confusing indeed. Possibly in some of your parishes next week there may be intense experiences of the Holy Spirit and the lives of you and some of your people may be gloriously revitalized. Pray God that may be so. But do not call it "Baptism," because so to call it is confused theology and also, I am convinced, spiritually divisive.

The gifts of the Spirit are many and St. Paul, in 1 Corinthians, describes the need for all of them in the building up of the Body of Christ. He would give no exclusive prominence or preeminence to the gift of speaking with tongues, but he gave exclusive prominence to the gift of love, charity, *agape,* the greatest gift of all.

There is, indeed, a contrast between the liveliness of the Apostolic Age, when it was exciting to be a Christian, with the miraculous gifts that were a part of that liveliness, not least the gifts of healing, and the sometimes dull, static character of contemporary church life. But just because the Spirit is the Spirit of Jesus, every gift that belongs to the life of Jesus himself is a mighty gift of the Holy Spirit — love, patience, wisdom, courage, self-sacrifice. And when we hear the words, "Ye shall do greater things than these," the greater works that the Apostles and their successors are going to do in Christ's name, we remember not only how Christ healed the sick, but also how, in patience and love, he could use suffering and let suffering be transfigured. Let that gift not be forgotten — that when suffering overwhelms a Christian he can, in the power of Christ crucified, use it to be, in a creative way what reflects Christ's glory. "For you have not received the spirit of slavery to fall back again into fear, but you have received the spirit of sonship whereby we cry, 'Abba, Father.' It is the Spirit himself bearing witness with our spirit that we are children of God. And if children, then heirs of God and joint heirs with Christ, provided that if we suffer with him we shall also be glorified with him."

Glorified with him. This last phrase reminds us of an aspect of the Holy Spirit so fundamental that perhaps I ought to have mentioned it first of all, but let me close with it. Call it, if you will, the eschatalogical aspect of the Spirit. The Spirit is the first installment within our present life, of heaven which awaits us. The Holy Spirit is, in St. Paul's phrase the *arrabon*. In another phrase of St. Paul he is the "first fruits of our inheritance." In a phrase of St. Peter, he is "the Spirit of the glory." In the striking language of the Epistle to the Hebrews, the Christians are those who have "tasted the heavenly gift, become partakers of the Holy Spirit, tasted the goodness of the word of God and the powers of the age to come." In a word, the Spirit enables the Christian to live already in the perspective of heaven. He keeps this perspective of heaven alive in us as, day by day, he inspires us in the practical service of humanity. We do not indeed forget the relation of the Holy Spirit to suffering humanity, for we think of how the Messiah, at the opening of his ministry at the synagogue at Nazareth, said, "The Spirit of the Lord is upon me, because he has anointed me to preach good news to the poor, to proclaim release to the captives, recovering of sight to the blind, and to set at liberty the oppressed, and to proclaim the acceptable year of the Lord." But every act of love that the Spirit inspires and every prayer to the Father which the Spirit prompts are an anticipation already of heaven, where every act will be love and every word will be adoration. Faintly, unknowingly, the old writer of Ecclesiastes foreshadowed the apostolic doctrine of the Holy Spirit when he wrote the mysterious sentence: "He hath set eternity in their heart."

The Spirit and the Gospel of St. John

During the coming hour I invite you to visit with me in my home. And my home is the Gospel of St. John. We turn our thoughts to the Holy Spirit in the Fourth Gospel. The fourth Evangelist writes in the light of the considerable experience of the Holy Spirit in the first age of the Church. And at the same time, he relates that experience in the most intimate way to the person of our Lord himself. He thus leads us more deeply than any other New Testament writer into the inner relation of Christ, the Spirit, and the Church.

In the Fourth Gospel, as in the Synoptics, Jesus appears on the scene of history as the one on whom the Spirit rests and the one whose work it will be to bestow the Spirit, in due time, upon others. The Baptist was told, "He on whom you see the Spirit descend, the same is he who baptizes with the Holy Spirit."

Meanwhile, the old imagery of wind and water continues. In the conversation with Nicodemus in the night, Jesus speaks of the Spirit as wind, and the wind is going to accomplish through the Sacrament of Holy Baptism the new birth of Christian believers. And we notice the eschatalogical note, for a moment or two later Jesus says that as Moses lifted up the serpent in the wilderness, even so must the Son of Man be lifted up in order to be the source of eternal life. This power of the wind is going to turn upon the death and the exaltation of Jesus. Jesus also converses with the woman at Samaria by the well, and speaks to her of the living water, the water of the Holy Spirit. And again, looking toward eternity, he says that this water will be a well springing up into eternal life. But meanwhile, there is the same reticence about Spirit in the public teaching of Jesus. Reticence, but a mysterious reference, when Jesus is addressing the crowd in the city of Jerusalem as described in chapter seven: On the last day of the feast, the great day, Jesus stood and proclaimed, 'If any man thirst let him come to me and drink, and he who believes in me as the Scripture has said, out of his heart shall flow rivers of living water.' Now this he said about the Spirit, which those who believed of him were to receive; for as yet the Spirit had not been given because Jesus was not yet glorified."

In that single sentence, the Evangelist gives us the clue. The glory of Jesus must first be consummated in the passion and the resurrection, and only then can the Spirit be given to the disciples, for it will be the work of the Spirit to bring to the disciples the completed glory of Jesus so that it may be reproduced within them.

We pause here and ask what this glory meant. The glory of Jesus was the glory as of the only Son from the Father — as we read at the end of the prologue. The glory was the divine power and splendor shining in the world. But very soon, as the mission of Jesus proceeds, it becomes apparent that the power and splendor are the power and splendor of self-giving love. The Jews sought a glory of their own. Mankind seeks a glory, each person for himself. Jesus sought no glory of his own. He effaced himself in giving glory to the Father, while in turn the Father gave glory to him. And it was the glory of this self-giving love of eternal diety that was being disclosed in the mission of the Son on the soil of Palestine. Inevitably, there was a clash between this divine glory of self-giving love and glory as men understood it, the glory of prestige and power and self-assertion. The clash and the contrast are summed up in a single, tragic sentence of Jesus, chapter five, verse 44: "How can you believe, who receive glory one from another and the glory that comes from the only God, you do not seek?" Of course, men will not believe if they are so preoccupied with the glory that they heap upon one another, the false glory of power and prestige, that they do not recognize the glory of self-giving love when Jesus is bringing it into the world. Inevitably, then, the clash between the glory of God in Jesus, and the glory of man represented in his contemporaries, is inescapable, and it leads on to the passion. And the passion, as described by St. John, is on the one hand the enemies of Jesus getting their own way in destroying him, and on the other hand the divine glory having its own way, shining out more gloriously than ever in sacrifice and self-giving love. So the formula, "We saw his glory," applies to the passion as deeply as it applies to the Incarnation. For the passion, in John, is not a defeat needing the resurrection to reverse it. Rather it is a divine victory of love in glory so complete that the resurrection follows to set the seal upon it.

The first chapter in Christianity is thus the revealing of the glory in Jesus. The second chapter is the conveying of the glory to the disciples, and that is the supreme work of the Holy Spirit. "The glory which you have given to me, I have given to them that they may be one." It is in the discourse at the Last Supper that this future work of the Holy Spirit is fully drawn out. It would be impossible within our short time to mention all the facets of the teaching about glory. But, let me pick out the three most important. The Spirit will convict, the Spirit will be the Comforter, and the Spirit will be the spirit of truth. Convicting, comfort, truth. And by all these, the Spirit will glorify Jesus in the disciples.

First, the Spirit will convict. I quote the haunting words from St. John 16, "And he when he has come, will convict the world concerning sin, concerning righteousness, concerning judgment. Concerning sin, because they do not believe in me. Concerning righteousness because I go to the Father and ye will see me no more. Concerning judgment, because the ruler of this world is judged."

The world had, and still has radically wrong ideas, if it had any ideas at all, about three great realities — sin, righteousness, and judgment. Only the Holy Spirit, working in the consciences of men, can expose to them their error and bring them to the perception of what is true.

The imagery is partly that of the law court — marshaling the evidence, proving the case, establishing the guilt, dealing out the penalty. But the imagery of the law court seems to pass into the imagery of personal persuasion; the winning of the mind and the conscience from one view to the other, so that the one whom the evidence has condemned comes himself to accept and be an exponent of the very truth he had rejected. About sin — "About sin in that they believe not in me" — those words seem harsh, but the rejection of Jesus was a moral issue. Jesus was not rejected because of the conscientiousness of intellectual skepticism. He was rejected because his contemporaries were were preoccupied with the self-centered, self-protective glory of man in such a way that they were blind to the glory of God, even though the glory of God was there present for their eyes to see.

"About righteousness, in that I go to the Father and ye see me no more." When Jesus left the world to go to his death, the world thought that one more imposter was done away with, one more figure who had caused a great stir passing out into a kind of limbo of irrelevance. But no; the truth was that when Jesus went out to disappear in death, it was the supreme righteous act — righteous love and obedience doing its supreme work — and the righteousness of God's servant was vindicated by the Father in raising him from death.

As for judgment, when Jesus died, the world thought that Jesus was being judged if ever a man was judged — judged by the Sanhedren, judged by the Roman power, judged by the condemnation of popular opinion, judged apparently by God himself — for cursed is the man who hangs on the tree. But in truth, Jesus was himself the judge and Calvary is the divine judgment on every contemporary participant in the event. And it is the divine judgment on every civilization unto the end of time, the judgment upon all our ways of life and all our cultures. And on each of these issues — sin, righteousness, and judgment — the mind of the world was and still is utterly wrong. It is the supernatural work of the Holy Spirit to expose in hearts and minds the depth of error and to bring hearts and minds to the conviction of the truth.

We preach the Christian faith; we engage in mission and apologetics; we confront the world with the Christian message. But amidst all our intellectual, and social, and pastoral activity should there not be a great deal more prayer that the Holy Spirit will use our little efforts in the convicting of hearts and minds and consciences? We prepare our sermons and preach them, but it is the work of the convicting Spirit in us, and in our hearts to make the message strike home to them. And would that we recovered, through our pastoral, evangelistic, and apologetic ministry, this belief that he who matters supremely is the convicting Spirit. While the Spirit convicts the world, enough of the world lingers in us, in our own dreadful sinfulness, that we, if we are to be faithful, need again and again to be convicted by the Spirit.

The instrument by which the Spirit convicts us is the instrument of the cross. The *Veni Creator* and the crucifix go together.

The Spirit who convicts also comforts. The word *Paraclete* now comes into view. Its most obvious meaning is "advocate," one who pleads a cause. The Spirit will plead the cause of divine truth against those who oppose it or ignore it. But the advocacy of the Spirit is not confined to the marshaling of the arguments for Christianity, for alongside the work of apologetics and exposition of the supreme "case" for Christianity is the existence of Christians who live in the way of holiness. The Spirit enables us to be witnesses who show in the court of history and conscience that the Christian way is true. We shall not cease from the witness of intellectual discussion and persuasion, for it is part of the Spirit's work, but we may suspect that two or three saintly lives may prove as much as many books and pamphlets.

Besides the translation "advocate" the word

Paraclete is also translated "comforter." There have
been those who shrink from this translation through
a feeling that it suggests something cozy. But the
root idea is the doctrine of the divine comfort we
find in the book of Isaiah and in some of the
Psalms. "Comfort ye, comfort ye, my people, saith
your God." The Lord shall comfort Zion. It is the
doctrine that in the last days God will come and
comfort his people. This comfort will include the
banishing of enemies from the land and the
bringing of peace. It will include prosperity, good
harvests — corn and wine and oil — and the people
will be happy and secure. But it also includes the
extirpation of injustice and wrongdoing, and the
coming of God's righteousness, and the doing of
God's will. In a word, all the blessings and demands
of messianic salvation, that is, the divine comfort
coming to Israel. Such is the comfort that the Spirit
will bring to the disciples in a more intimate and
more inward way. It will be joy, the joy of which
Christ spoke to the Apostles in the upper room. It
will be peace, the peace that Christ brings into the
souls of disciples, utterly different from the peace
the world seeks. And all in terms of God's forgiveness and the doing of God's will.

Thus, the divine comfort and the divine
conviction always go together. They are like the
opposite sides of a single coin. I quote E. C.
Hoskyns again: "The Spirit of Truth, just because he
reveals God's love and assures man of it, himself
exposes the darkness and blindness of the world.
The consolation of the disciples is consolation in
the midst of condemnation; and if the word

comforter secures recognition of the boundless mercy, the word *advocate* secures recognition of the sternness of the issue."

The role of the Spirit as Spirit of truth recurs in the discourse. He will guide the disciples into all the truth, he will teach them all things, he will remind them of the things Jesus said, he will show them the things that are coming. And this work of the Spirit of truth seems to be interwoven with the other aspects of the Spirit's work. And no wonder, for Jesus himself is the truth, as well as the way and the life. The Spirit of truth will both guide the disciples toward the future and recall the past to them. The things Jesus revealed to the disciples, both at the Supper and in his whole mission, could not be fully understood at once. But in the course of time, the Spirit would bring to the disciples a greater understanding. The message of Jesus will be unfolded in the coming years.

This process of growing illumination through the guidance of the Holy Spirit is illustrated in the varieties of Christian thought within the Apostolic Age. Thus, the doctrine of the cosmic role of Christ in Colossians, the theme of the high priesthood of Christ in Hebrews, the place of Christ in the cataclysmic drama of world history in the Apocalypse — all these are instances of the Spirit taking the things of Christ and unfolding them to the Church. Indeed, the Fourth Gospel itself is, as a whole, an example of this process, as significant as any in history.

Does the process close with the first century? No, for the Spirit in every age is able to bring to the

Church new understanding of Christ's revelation of God in relation to the world he has created. Again and again, new intellectual movements have been used by the Spirit of truth to bring greater understanding of the Christian revelation. I think we should all agree that a significant instance of that took place in the intellectual revolution in the last century. It first seemed that the new sciences of evolutionary biology and historical criticism were damaging to the authority of the Bible. But the Spirit of truth showed how both those sciences can be used, not to mar, but rather to illuminate the Christian's belief in the process of the divine creation of the world and in his progressive revelation of God in diverse ways through the writers of Holy Scripture.

While, however, the Spirit will lead the disciples along the way of truth, that way, the *hodos,* is Christ himself. The unfolding work of the Spirit includes therefore the ceaseless witnessing of the Church to Christ himself. The promise of guidance into all truth is linked with the disciples' faithfulness to something already given to them. Thus, the Spirit will remind the disciples of the things Jesus said. He will bear witness to Jesus and enable them to bear witness to Jesus by conserving what Jesus himself did and taught in the days of his ministry. Indeed, the Spirit's mission is explicitly linked with the obedience of the disciples to Jesus' own commands and the guarding by the disciples of Jesus' own words. It is the things of Jesus which the Spirit will take and declare to the Apostles and declare to the Church in every age.

Very significantly, what the Spirit will declare is "the things that are coming" and may not those words refer to what was imminently coming — the death and the resurrection? It is as the Church is faithful to the centrality of the death and resurrection of a supernatural Savior, and only thus, that the Spirit will be guiding the Church into greater apprehensions of the truth in successive ages.

In those ways, the Spirit will glorify Jesus in the disciples, by convicting, by comforting, by being the Spirit of truth. In all these ways the Spirit effaces himself in glorifying Christ just as Christ effaces himself in glorifying the Father.

It seems to me doubtful whether the power of the Spirit, any more than the power of Christ or the power of the Father, is going to be measured by our human awareness. In our Christian life, there are many moments of awareness: awareness of oneself, awareness of one's neighbors, awareness of one or other of the persons of the blessed Trinity, awareness sometimes of the unspeakable greatness of the triune God. But awareness is surely never a test of spirituality, and to make it so may lead us into great misunderstandings. In the whole of his work, reproducing the glory of Jesus in Christian disciples, the Spirit leads us to join with Christ himself in glorifying the Father.

In the remaining few minutes of our time, I turn to the relation of the Holy Spirit, beyond the Church, to the created world. It belongs to the doctrine of John's prologue that the divine Logos is at work in all creation, giving life to nature and light to mankind in every race and culture, far beyond the sphere of the biblical revelation. And St. John's doctrine is in line with the Jewish teaching about the divine wisdom at work in all the world, and at work in humanity, changing men into friends of God and prophets. In the New Testament writings, the word "Spirit" is used exclusively for spirit within the Christian community and is not used for this wider activity of God in the created world. No doubt the new experience of Holy Spirit in the Christian community was so vivid and tremendous that it was natural to use the word only for those things that were happening through Jesus and the New Covenant. Nonetheless, the Apostles knew that the whole world, darkened by sin though it was, is the scene of the activity of God, who created it.

St. Paul, in the Epistle to the Romans, in the midst of the most terrible denunciation of the sins of the Gentile world, affirms that God may be known to man in nature and in conscience, far beyond the borders of either the old or the new covenants. "Ever since the creation of the world, God's invisible nature, namely, his eternal power and diety, has been clearly perceived in the things that he has made so that they are without excuse." The world is full of altars to unknown gods. And if altars to unknown gods witness even to the smallest fragments of truth, we Christians acknowledge those fragments as evidence that the divine word is, indeed, at work in all creation — the light that lightens every man.

We face here a vast problem, and Christian theology has again and again oscillated between those who have dwelt upon the depravity of the human race and given little recognition to the doctrine of the light that lightens every man, and those, on the other hand, who put so much emphasis on the light that lightens every man as, perhaps, to obscure, in a broad Christian humanism, the uniqueness of salvation through Christ crucified. Let me mention two fields in which the relation between the gospel and the strivings of the human conscience and mind outside the borders of the Church are, at this time, significant.

First, there is the striving for liberty and justice. We, who are Christians, cannot be indifferent to that striving, at least when we remember the mission of the Messiah in the synagogue at Nazareth: "The spirit of the Lord is upon me because he has anointed me to preach good news to the poor and to proclaim release to the captives." A Church that allows itself to be identified with worldly power and comfort and the privileges of the economic status-quo is not a Church that is going to be listened to by those whose consciences are stirred about justice. Yet I believe that attempts to identify Christian salvation with political revolution are misleading. In his recent book, *The Political Christ,* Dr. Alan Richardson analyzes this problem, and I think he shows convincingly that what are called theologies of liberation very often rest upon a superficial exigesis and a misreading of the relation of Jesus himself to the zealots and other contemporary movements. We cannot identify the gospel with political liberation, because the gospel is concerned not with a less radical but with a more radical liberation — the liberation of man himself into eternal life in union with God. Nonetheless, this radical gospel of delivering man into union with God in eternal life will not be conveyed except by a Church that is deeply sensitive to situations of human suffering and is ceaselessly engaged in the service of those who suffer and in upholding the cause of justice in Christ's name.

A second aspect of the problem is the relation of Christianity to the sciences. Again it is for us, as Christians, to perceive the hand of God at work in the sciences, to be learning truth from every genuine science, and to be using what we thus learn in the service of the gospel. It seems likely that we shall hear more in the future of sciences that bear upon the understanding and manipulation of human beings. There are developments that cause us to ask what may be their effect upon man as a free being, and upon the realities of conscience, of right and wrong, of sin, and grace and holiness.

In this area which is scientifically difficult, but also of great pastoral importance, I make only one comment. I believe that a crucial area is that which is called "clinical." In our pastoral ministrations, we are bound to be drawing upon clinical, therapeutic wisdom. But there is a world of difference between mental and physical health and wholeness and the holiness, the saintliness, the Christ-likeness that are our concern as Christian pastors. There are today too many Christians, and sometimes too many priests and counselors, who confuse the two. The whole man, the hundred percent man — in mind and body — is one thing. But another thing is the saintly man or woman, whose strength *may* be perfected in one hundred percent wholeness, but *may* also be perfected, like the saintliness of a St. Paul, amidst weakness and suffering. It is saints whom the Holy Spirit creates, and it is saints who point to the glory of Jesus. It is in order to become saints and nothing else that you and I were baptized in the Baptism of our Christian initiation.

We who are Christians live the life of the Spirit in the midst of a bewildering and cruel world. There have been, and there are, bold Christian thinkers who, inspired by St. John's doctrine of the Logos, have attempted a synthesis of God, the world, the evolutionary process, with Christ and his death and resurrection as a key to the whole. In our own times, the noblest attempt at such a synthesis was made by Teilhard de Chardin, who saw the whole process of the world, scientifically and mystically, with Christ as the origin, Christ as the goal, and Christ mystically present in every stage of the process. But if our minds are not capable of finding a synthesis of such a kind, or if our minds are filled with a certain skepticism about the possibility of such a synthesis, we need not be afraid. The great thing is that, as Christians possessing the Holy Spirit, we walk by faith, and walking by faith we believe that the key to the meaning of this world is the death and resurrection of our Lord, which is his glory. And when the Holy Spirit reproduces in us only a tiny part of that glory, he assures us that the

world is in the hands of a faithful Creator, and we
already have a foretaste of the heaven for which he
created us.

Leon-Joseph Cardinal Suenens

Archbishop of Malines-Brussels

The Holy Spirit
and the Church

My dear brothers and sisters in the Lord, it is a great joy to be with you again this year, as I was last year, both here in New York and San Francisco. Last year I told you that on returning to the States I was impressed with something new in your country. A kind of message was coming from your country to the world — a message telling us that God was not dead, in spite of what had been said a few years ago, and that Jesus was not a myth, in spite of all the theological rumors about that. And your youth was proclaiming in different ways that

Jesus is the Lord and the Saviour. At the same time, you were telling us something else, that the Holy Spirit was alive again in an unexpected way. The Holy Spirit is always surprising and unexpected but now something new was growing and blossoming. A sort of new springtime for the Holy Spirit was coming; that was what I told you last year. Today and tomorrow I wish to speak more profoundly of that presence of the Spirit for the Church and the world of today.

I am always very impressed when I open the Scriptures and especially St. Paul's Letter to the Corinthians and I read how the Holy Spirit is there, playing a very realistic role. He is there, leading the Apostles, pushing them, telling them what to do, where to go, where not to go, bringing them together, speaking to them in gatherings, making his presence felt among them so that they can truly say that it is the Holy Spirit who speaks, works and acts through them. Really the Acts of the Apostles are the Acts of the Holy Spirit. So when I read the letters of St. Paul I feel that on every page the Spirit is there at work.

Then something happened in the Church of God. What we saw there in the beginning of the history of the Church seemed to disappear or at least to come under a sort of shadow. We can still trace those gifts of the Spirit down through the ages and through the centuries, but they became a kind of monopoly for saints and monks. You find it in the oriental tradition, yes. And you find it today, but you do not have the impression that we are still in the same fullness of the Spirit of God. What has been happening over the last few years, starting here in the States, is that a new awareness of the fullness and the living reality of the Spirit is coming to us again. And I should say coming in the fullness of his gifts. We have, of course, always received gifts of the Spirit, and out of these gifts come the fruits of the Spirit, but we had become more or less shy in front of the Spirit. We accepted *some* of the Spirit and we pushed aside others as if they were outmoded. What we are discovering today in the Charismatic Renewal of the Church, is really a new awareness of the fullness of the gifts of the Spirit. As I read again what St. Paul had to say to the early Christians, I have to confess and testify that what he says is also for the Church today. It is not for past history that St. Paul says,

> In each of us the Spirit is manifested in one particular way for some useful purpose. One man through the Spirit has the gift of wise speech, while another by the same power of the Spirit can. put the deepest knowledge into words. Another by the same Spirit is granted faith; another by the one Spirit, the gift of healing; another miraculous powers; another has the gift of prophecy; and another has the ability to distinguish true spirits from false. Yet another has the gift of ecstatic utterance of different kinds, and another the ability to interpret it. But all these gifts are from the one and same Spirit who distributes them separately to each individual at will. 1 Corinthians 12:7-11

Is this just something said for the past or is this "actuality"? Well, I think that it is "actuality" in the renewal of today called the Charismatic Renewal. I should really prefer the term "Renewal in the Holy Spirit" as that is really what it is. We must clarify the vocabulary. For instance, I am not too pleased when we speak of the "Baptism in the Spirit" unless one explains very clearly what one means. It is really the release, the coming to full freedom and liberty of all those gifts of the Spirit which we have already received at our Baptism and Confirmation. It is not any sort of new sacrament but rather a revitalization of those gifts of the Spirit until now hidden within us and now coming to openness, to full blossoming.

In this renewal in the Church today we have a new awareness of the full spectrum of the gifts of the Holy Spirit. We must not be afraid to accept the Spirit with all its manifestations, just as we find them in the gospels and St. Paul. We must not be afraid of accepting that the Holy Spirit is today manifesting himself in the same ways. We must open our faith to that. What is needed from each of us today is what I should call an "expectant faith." In order to receive the gifts of God, we must *expect* them, be open to them. And in the measure that we are "expectantly" open to him, the Holy Spirit can accomplish all those wonders that we read about at the beginning of the Church. Each one of us needs that expectant faith. Come Holy Spirit! I do not ask of you any special gift but neither do I refuse any either, because we receive those manifestations not for ourselves but for the kingdom of God, for the building up of His church. One will receive a certain manifestation of the Spirit, another a different one, but all will use their particular gifts to share in the upbuilding of your Church. This is Charismatic reality and at the same time visible and sacramental reality.

We bishops received the Spirit in the episcopacy and we received the Spirit in the priesthood, in the different ministries we received there. One of the nicest definitions of a bishop I heard here yesterday. A bishop is one who receives the charism to discern charisms, to guide them and bind them together. This is another aspect of this new awareness today, of the full spectrum of the gifts of the Spirit. When I say the full spectrum, it is not only the list given by St. Paul. In two or three places he has given us different lists. We cannot list all the gifts of the Spirit, for the Spirit is at work in full radiance. Like the countless rays of the sun, you have a whole spectrum of gifts available to you in that new awareness of the Holy Spirit at work today. "Come Holy Spirit with *all* Your manifestations." We are ready to receive them even if they are disturbing because we know that we, as shepherds of the Church, will have the gift to discern them. We must accept that full play of the gifts of the Spirit. I would compare it to playing an organ. You can play the organ with one finger or with one hand or with two. You can play it with all its variety, high and low, leaving all the register open, letting the wind come and play through all the pipes. The invitation of today is like that; nothing new but rather something renewed. The full play, the full breeze of the Spirit is blowing in the world and helping us to accept it. I think this is the first of our duties, to "expect" the gifts of the Spirit. "And it will be given to you according to your faith." This is in the gospel. As a church, as a community, we will receive those gifts. We need them and we will receive them and it will be such a great thing for the church in the world.

What is also new, and you understand that by now I mean renewed, is not only this awareness of the fullness of the spectrum of gifts, but also a renewed faith in the power of the Spirit. And if power is needed any time, it is needed more than ever today. We feel weak, perhaps discouraged, because there is such a disproportion between what we have to do and our weakness. We are weak instruments in God's hands to bring the gospel, to make Christ alive in this world today. Look at the people in the streets! What are they searching for? Are they not searching, unconsciously perhaps, for the deepest meaning of their life? God is there, but only in the shadow. We have to do a disproportionate work. Bringing the gospel to the world of today needs power. And the Holy Spirit is there once again with his power, with the fullness of his power, especially in his ministry.

I am always impressed by the consecration of a bishop. In our ritual we have very strong words. "Holy Spirit, come into this man so that he can accomplish the ministry of reconciliation and be able to do signs and wonders." We receive the power to do miracles, wonders of God, in a visible or invisible way. It is the logic of the Word of the Lord who said: "I will leave you, but I will come again and you will do greater things than I." Greater, because he will do them through his Spirit in us.

We must be conscious, bishops and priests, of the power we receive by our ordination. We are powerful men. On one condition — that *we* disappear. We are powerful in the measure of our humility, in the measure that we do not speak on our own. The world is not interested in what *we* say but the world is interested in what God is thinking. He needs prophets, he needs people speaking in his name, saying "You are powerful Christians. Do not be afraid. I am there. I am with you on the road."

This is another view. We Christians are all of us overshadowed by that Spirit of God, on the day of our Baptism, on the day we were baptized in the Spirit, which means in the *power* of God. Even the name we bear, Christians, means anointed by the Spirit. The first Christians could have been called the "followers of Jesus," "the companions of Jesus," even "Jesuits." We missed that! We received the name "Christians," anointed by the spirit, in the power of the Spirit.

And thinking about Jesus himself, see how often in the Gospel it speaks of Jesus armed with the power of the Holy Spirit, going to Galilee, going to Nazareth. Remember the scene when he opened the scroll in the synagogue and found the text: "The Spirit of the Lord is upon me because he has anointed me." This is essential. After reading that, go and preach the gospel. Not only in words, but take all the social problems in hand and take them in the power of the Spirit, not just on the purely sociological level. We have something more profound and powerful, the wisdom of the Spirit and the power of the Spirit. Now I should say, let our faith be more courageous. We need courageous faith just because we are confirmed in the strength of the Spirit, knowing that faith means openness to the power of the Spirit. I see the image of that expectant faith, of that courageous faith, in Mary. No one "expected" the Spirit of God like Mary, the mother of God. No one was overshadowed by the power of the Spirit like Mary. She gave Christ to the world in that extraordinary, expectant and courageous faith, walking in the darkness of faith. We ask her and we ask all the apostles — all those who preceeded us in faith — that our faith should be more and more expectant faith and courageous faith.

Going a step further, I should say that what is new today is a renewed awareness of the presence of the Holy Spirit as an actuality of today. If our faith were stronger we should discern that presence much more than we do. We need expectant faith, we need courageous faith and we need discerning faith to see and feel and experience the Spirit at work. He is there, among us as the most real reality, the most real person. Remember Jesus said: "Where two or three are gathered together in my name, I am there in the midst of you through my Spirit." You are gathered here in the name of the Lord so that you may tomorrow better testify to the Christian message. He is here speaking to you through everything here, even through the speaker. Because he will tell you something that I am not even thinking about. He will use such and such a word to give you his message. I will not even know what that message will be. But I just pray to him: "Holy Spirit, come, tell them what you wish." It is a dialogue with him that you are searching for here.

So discerning faith means seeing Christ where he is, seeing the Spirit where he is, and in that new awareness of the Spirit, you will find Christ and the Spirit in some privileged places. You will find them in the community where you are praying together. You will find in a very special way the presence of Christ and of the Spirit in prayer groups. You will find them when you are coming together to pray in his name. You will find them in a very special way in Holy Scripture. Jesus promised us that he would send us the Spirit to introduce us to the fullness of his gospel. He said very clearly, "You do not understand yet all I have to say. I will send you the Spirit who will introduce you to the depths of my words." The Spirit will explain the scriptures to you in a unique way. That is what Jesus did to the two disciples at Emmaus when he went with them on the road, opening their eyes to understand the scriptures from the beginning, from Moses to the moment of his resurrection. It was Jesus revealing himself behind those words of holy scripture. That kind of conversation of Jesus with the disciples at Emmaus continues today, for each of us. The Holy Spirit will tell us about Jesus in every line of the gospel helping us to understand it with his understanding.

There are two ways of reading it. The first way is just to know what the inspired writer is saying. We have to discover the objective meaning of what he is saying and we need all the exegetical sciences to clarify all that. That is useful, but it is just one way of reading scripture, what I should call a general and absolutely preliminary one. But then we have the right to open the gospel and ask the Lord to give us our daily bread. Just as I find the presence of the Lord in the Eucharist under the appearance of bread and wine, he is there, too, under the appearance of all those words said for all humanity, said for all time, but said also for you and me today in a very special way.

I am always impressed by the fact that Jesus came into the synagogue and they brought him the scrolls of the Old Testament. He opened them at random and found exactly his vocation depicted there. "The Spirit of God is upon me, this is what I am, this is my identity." So we should open the gospel in that spirit of faith, asking the Spirit to enlighten us, to give us a consciousness of his presence, meaning that he is very near speaking softly. You have to be silent to hear what he is saying to you through the text. After the first reading it can have another sense. I found this when I had a problem and I asked myself what I should do, should I go and speak, or should I keep silent? It is much easier to do nothing and to keep silent. Should I go and speak, with the danger of making a bit of trouble perhaps? I opened the gospel and I found the text said to St. Paul by the Spirit: "Go to Jerusalem and speak and tell what you have to say." Well, of course, I do not have to go to Jerusalem. I understand perfectly what it means. Go to Rome! But it is said in a different way.

I hope the Archbishop will not mind if I tell this story of what happened to us when he spent a few days at my house in Malines. This is where the memorable "Conversationes" of Malines, over which Cardinal Mercier presided, took place. Before starting our talks I suggested that we pray together and that we open the gospel to see what the Lord had to tell us. You can imagine the scene, the Primate of England and the Cardinal of Belgium asking the Lord, through the gospel, "Tell us, if you like. We do not have the right to insist, but it would be nice to know!" We opened the gospels and found the text of St. John, and the text was this: "In spite of the fact that the doors were shut, Jesus came and stood among them and said 'Peace be with you!' " It seemed to us that this was an invitation of the Lord to continue our dialogue despite the closed doors, knowing in our hearts that the Lord, true to his word, was truly there with us because we were gathered in his name. Well, I think the doors are closed in a way but they are unlocked and the windows are open! and the Holy Spirit is saying to us that even though this morning you cannot change the doors and the walls, let us be at peace. Let us go forward together on the road towards unity.

As I am telling you stories, let me tell you another one, just to show what it means to be constantly aware of the presence of the Lord in our daily life. However, let me warn you! You will not always find such a perfect answer when you open the scriptures. You could open it at the index or even at the descriptions of the buildings of the temple of Jerusalem. I did that one day while praying with some friends. I opened the scriptures at the description of the temple of Jerusalem. My reaction was that it was perfectly useless, but one of the others said, "Oh, isn't it wonderful, how interested God is in the smallest detail of his creatures, listing for us all the details in order to teach us respect for God." Yes, God is really there in the smallest details of human life. The more our faith becomes a discerning faith, the more we will see his presence.

When I look back at my life, I am always struck when I see how many times God has helped me in striking ways; by a book sent to me by someone, by a note, by an article read at exactly the moment I needed it, by a phone call, by the visit of someone coming from the other side of the world to tell you something; God is there behind all those incidents. As in the garden on Easter morning, you cannot always recognize him, but he is there. He is there. He is there in each one of those details and the more your faith grows, the more you will see it. "If you believe in me, you will see the glory of God," said Jesus. If you believe, you will see the glory of God in your own life, in your own vocation, the story you alone can tell.

For example. He brought you here. Why are you here? Why am I here? It is not the ordinary thing. It is a very unexpected play of the Spirit. I think the Spirit of God is writing novels that are ten thousand times better than we could write. He has a lot of imagination. He is writing the life of each of you, in very unexpected ways. You must open your soul with discerning faith to what he is doing in your daily life.

But I promised you a story which is full of meaning for me and you can perhaps translate it into your own life in other circumstances. Two or three years ago I celebrated the 25th anniversary of my consecration as a bishop. That morning I was struggling with a problem . . . something about going to Jerusalem . . . and my problem was, should I speak or not. I had to give an interview about the implementation of Vatican II and how we should go forward on the way of coresponsibility. Is it wise to speak even if the circumstances are not the best and there is the risk of being misunderstood? That was my problem. So I went into my library and I noticed that there was a book out of place. As I took the book to return it to the shelf, I looked at it and it was *The Journal of a Soul* by Pope John. So I stopped and said: "Well, Pope John, today is the 25th anniversary of my consecration as a bishop. You were always so nice and so good to me during your life. I don't ask it, but I think it would be nice if you had something to tell me from this book on the journal of your soul. I opened the book and I found these lines:

On the day of my episcopal consecration the Church gave me a particular mandate concerning it: 'Let him choose humility and truth and never forsake them for any flattery or threats. Let him not consider light to be darkness, or darkness light; let him not call evil good, or good evil. Let him learn from wise men and fools, so that he may profit from all.' I thank the Lord for having given me a natural inclination to tell the truth, always and in all circumstances and before everyone, in a pleasant manner and with courtesy, to be sure, but calmly and fearlessly. Certain small fibs of my childhood have left in my heart a horror of deceit and falsehood. Now, especially as I am growing old, I want to be particularly careful about this: to love the truth, God helping me! I have repeated this many times, swearing it on the gospel.

This was the message of Pope John for me and it has helped me. I said simply, "Thank you."

I wish to conclude by saying that in the Charismatic Renewal of today there is a call for each one of us. Let us be open to the Spirit's visitation. It is very much like what happened in the Old Testament ... God is visiting his people. It is not always in the same way but from time to time he does show himself to us in a very striking way. Let us be open and expectant! Let us be strong and firm in our faith, believing that faith can move mountains. Let us ask for the grace of seeing the presence of the Spirit in every circumstance, knowing that he is very near to each one of us. Thank you.

The Holy Spirit
and Unity

O Lord, may we hear, as if we had never heard them before, the words you spoke to your apostles. Let us hear them with an open heart and mind and soul. Jesus said: "I am praying for those who put their faith in me, that they may all be one; even as thou, Father, art in me, and I in thee, that they also may be in us, so that the world may believe that thou has sent me. The glory which thou hast given me I have given to them, that they may be one even as we are one, I in them and thou in me, that they may become perfectly one . . ."

My dear friends, I pray with you to try to understand in the light of the Spirit the mystery of unity, of growing together, of being together, the mystery of being in communion in depth.

Tonight the image that comes to my mind is the image of the Trinity, the Father in the Son, totally Father and totally giving Himself; and the Son, totally Son, and the total expression of the Father, in that fusion of being one in that eternal love. This is the image we must keep in mind if we are to become pilgrims together travelling towards that unity which the Lord gave us as a mandate. Let us examine that image more closely in order that we might better understand what we have to do.

Yesterday the Archbishop quoted from a very profound book by John Taylor, published last year under the striking title *The Go-Between God*. The Holy Spirit is the "go-between"; the "go-between" between Father and the Son, and between Son and the Father; being their mutual love, their mutual reciprocity. This is the Holy Spirit at work.

A very simple man once told me, "You know that love between my wife and me is such a strong thing that we have no difficulty understanding that in God, love is a person." The Holy Spirit, the "go-between" is the living "go-between" creating communion, a binding force, in spite of all that can divide us. It is about that binding force that we wish to meditate together today.

We find in the Spirit unity and plurality at the same time. There is plurality in that unity and unity in that plurality. There is no uniformity. It is the fullness of the Father, of the Son and of the Spirit.

Let us look at that image, that oneness in plurality. In a way we could say about God that he has to be three to be God. This image of the Trinity can be a sort of guideline in our ecumenical striving to obtain, by the grace of God, but also by working and praying together, that visible unity of love shining forth among us. "Oh Lord, pray for us, because we so strongly need someone to be our go-between, to bring us from this level of coexistence to a new stage of communion."

We must travel on many different levels on the way from co-existence to communion. I wish to start on the level of the family, or rather on the level of the union which exists between wife and husband. I think the Holy Spirit is at work there in a very special way today. There is a sort of charismatic renewal of marriage, a new creation of communication between wife and husband and I think it is worthwhile that we should speak about it.

The intention to speak about this came to me yesterday when I heard an associate of Dr. Terwilliger speak about something called Marriage Encounter. What is Marriage Encounter? It is essentially a way of bringing husbands and wives to a deeper love and understanding of one another. It is not a method of bringing bad marriages to renewal, nor is it a method of solving problems in marriage. The purpose of a "Marriage Encounter" is to give fresh life to love in marriage and to renew, through a deeper understanding of its meaning, the bond between husband and wife. So often there is such a lack of real communication between couples, even in good solid marriages. Over a period of years, married life can become a routine co-existence, with each spouse so preoccupied with their own duties that no time is left for the deep sharing of each others personal lives and feelings. If married love is to be genuine it must be a communion of soul, spirit, heart and body.

Communion of soul means that life is really shared in its depth, and that both partners are able to mutually communicate what is deepest within them. Communion of spirit means deep oneness in the way they both look at life and its fundamental problems. St. Exupery wrote: "To love is not to gaze at each other, but to look outward, together, in the same direction." Communion of hearts means mutual affection, gift of self, sharing in full the existence of the other. Communion of body means physical union as the bodily expression of the sentiments of the soul.

The tragedy of the world today is that it disrupts and disintegrates the essential harmony of these elements and puts such a stress on the physical dimension that love becomes a caricature and nothing more than a juxtaposition of egoisms. In a word, love must be saved from all that threatens it, and love must be rediscovered deep in the heart of man.

This is the objective to which "Marriage Encounter" tries to respond and its success is impressive. Its method is a week end retreat under the direction of two or three married couples and a priest. The teaching given embraces all that is sound in human experience and psychology and the sharing is not a common sharing but is only between husband and wife. The retreat is followed up by periodic meetings together. This movement has its ecumenical dimension as couples of different denominations attend the retreats. There are Episcopal expressions of Marriage Encounter and now encounters of this kind are also being held among our Jewish brethren.

One realizes here to what extent the Holy Spirit, the living bond between Father and Son, is also the bond between husband and wife. It is he who brings to life the sacramental grace of marriage, bestowing on it a charismatic quality. Testimonies abound of married couples who have found again at a new depth, their unity in the Spirit, and who have come away from these weekends with a wholly new outlook and a wholly new joy, sure signs of the Spirit. I have heard many of these testimonies myself since the movement has been introduced into my diocese. Over two thousand couples in Belgium have already had the experience of this renewal. I can only affirm that the finger of God is there; that a breath of spring is blowing over the wide field of family life which badly needs to be renewed and lived in a truly Christian climate. The Holy Spirit is there, the go-between for husband and wife in the family.

Just as we have seen the action of the Holy Spirit in marriage between husband and wife so we see him, in a much larger dimension, as go-between among Christians today. In the Charismatic Renewal we see him uniting Christians of all persuasions. Those on the extreme right and those on the extreme left have not only found each other but the wonder of it is that they love one another. They encounter each other on a deeper level, the level of the Spirit. It is not just human love, it is the love of the Spirit. We are loving with his love so that, even though differences of opinion remain, yet in depth there is unity. I am struck by this because even though there is such polarization among Christians today, in the Charismatic Renewal he is there at the center.

I remember a journalist asked me one time, "As a Christian, are you to the right or to the left?" I answered, remembering the words of the famous theologian, John Courtney Murray, "I am extreme center." I believe the Holy Spirit is the extreme center in depth. That is an indication of the presence of the Spirit as go-between among Christians and especially as go-between in the renewal of ministry. Even though there is a shortage of priests in the Church today, something new is emerging. This is the mission of the Spirit on the parish level. The Spirit works in our daily lives in the conscience of every Christian activating the charismatic gifts already there. The building up of the Body of Christ should be done together with all God's people using the charisms they have received to their fullest potential. Bishops and priests have been given the gift of discerning charisms so that like symphony directors they will be able to bring together and to harmonize all of these charisms for the benefit of the body of Christ in their parishes and dioceses. I think something wonderful is happening here.

Much humility is needed on the part of priests

who are accustomed to working in their ministry almost alone. The laity, too, will need humility to accept that mutual correction of each other in order that the building up of the Body of Christ can be accomplished. I think we are on the eve of a wonderful Charismatic renewal of our whole community and especially of our parishes.

On Sunday when I leave, I expect to go to the parish of Christ the Redeemer in Houston, Texas. Though I have not yet seen it in action, I have met some of the parishioners and I have a feeling that the Charismatic Renewal is developing there in a splendid way. So many of their parishioners are accepting their full Christian responsibility. They not only bring the gospel to all but they translate it into action, so that God's words take on real meaning in service to one another in that part of the world. I see this as the new orientation for the future: The Holy Spirit, the Go-between, first between husband and wife, then spreading to all Christians, developing them into communities based on real Christian love. I see a new wave of Christians bound together by this powerful Go-Between.

Perhaps, in the past, we have forgotten that one of the first duties of Christians is to be "one" so that the world seeing this example of unity among Christians, will receive Christ's message of love to the world. I think we have come to a warmer realization as to what Christian community means. Just read the letters of St. Paul and notice the special attention he gives to each person. What warmth there is, what a truly personal relationship! He speaks of each member of every community because he knows and loves them. To the Roman community he wrote:

> I commend to you our sister Phoebe, a deaconess of the church at Cenchreae. Give her, in union with the Lord, a welcome worthy of saints, and help her with anything she needs: she has looked after a great many people, myself included.
>
> My greetings to Prisca and Aquila, my fellow workers in Christ Jesus, who risked death to save my life: I am not the only one to owe them a debt of gratitude, all the churches among the pagans do as well. My greetings also to the church that meets at their house.
>
> Greetings to my friend Epaenetus, the first of Asia's gifts to Christ; greetings to Mary who worked so hard for you; to those outstanding apostles Andronicus and Junias, my compatriots and fellow prisoners who became Christians before me; to Ampliatus, my friend in the Lord; to Urban, my fellow worker in Christ; to my friend Stachys; to Apelles who has gone through so much for Christ; to everyone who belongs to the household of Aristobulus; to my compatriot Herodion; to those in the household of Narcissus who belong to the Lord; to Tryphaena and Tryphosa, who work hard for the Lord; to my friend Persis who has done so much for the Lord; to Rufus, a chosen servant of the Lord, and to his mother who has been a mother to me too. Greetings to Asyncritus, Phlegon, Hermes, Patrobas, Hermas, and all the brothers who are with them; to Philologus and Julia, Nereus and his sister, and Olympas and all the saints who are with them. Greet each other with a holy kiss. All the churches of Christ send greetings.

Unfortunately, our parishes are too large today to have that sort of warm community with all of the charisms at work. Hopefully some parishes will be renewed in a complete way by the total reception of the Charismatic Renewal as did this parish in

Houston and also others which have come to my notice. But even if in some parishes everyone does not join in, those who use their charismatic gifts can show what it means when the Holy Spirit brings together Christians in prayer and love. I think a wonderful work of the Spirit has begun and will continue to radiate throughout the Church.

Holy Spirit, go-between between wife and husband, go-between between Christian churches — and here we are confronted with the duty of Ecumenical unity. Let us not forget that once we were united. There was only one Church during the first thousand years. The first break was with the Oriental church and then later the Reformation. From the year one thousand to two thousand we have lived in a divided church. We are now at the eve of third millenium. I hope and pray that we will soon see visible unity. We must hope for this unity, not because it will make Christians more powerful but simply because the Lord asked us to do it. We must obey his will.

In the Roman Catholic Church, we started toward this goal very especially after Vatican II and at that moment Ecumenism was in the news and in the newspapers. There was an aura of expectation. After a while the news about Ecumenism became quieter and quieter. Some feel that it is in a state of depression. I do not believe that. It is only normal when something is beginning that you hear a great deal about it. It is something like riding in an airplane. When you are taking off you hear a lot of noise, but when you rise in the air, the noise dies down. You have the impression that you are not moving at all . . . but you *are* moving and from time to time there are some air pockets and the captain will occasionally tell you to fasten your seat belts. Well, let us believe in that flight. We are going nearer and nearer to Ecumenical unity on every level. I believe the first level of that growing together is in the Spirit of God. There is a Charismatic Renewal going on among the Christian churches, a Charismatic Renewal going across all the different denominations of the Christian Churches. I think it is important that when we speak about Charismatic Renewal we should see clearly what we have in mind. I was very glad to hear Archbishop Ramsey stress what I have in mind also. In speaking about the Charismatic Renewal we must be careful in our use of words. We must not use the words "baptism in the spirit" suggesting that this is a new sacrament. No. It is a *release* of what we have already received in our baptism and confirmation, now springing up, blossoming forth, flowering into the love that brings ordinary Christians together, praying and working in their daily lives.

It is very important to realize that to achieve ecumenical unity we must prepare for it faithfully in our everyday lives. Do you remember the sad outcome of the Council of Florence in the 15th century, in which unity between the Orthodox and Catholic church of Rome was accepted, confirmed, signed and sealed but never became effective. Why? Because the people were not prepared for it. It was something over their heads. On the level of our daily lives the Spirit must bring us together in prayer and holiness. This is essential.

I wish to recall with you the thoughts of your dear Archbishop when he spoke in New York about the task of ecumenical unity. He stressed that the problem is not to unite all our Churches just as they are. No. It means asking how may our Churches become more Christ like, more obedient to Christ's purpose for them. This is the question. It is not essentially a question of dialogue between the Church of Rome and the Church of Canterbury, nor is it a dialogue between the Church of Rome and the Church of Moscow. It is not a question of dialogue between the Churches mutually. It is a dialogue between each Church and Christ, under the impulse and emotion of the Spirit of God. We have to look to Jesus, to open the Gospel and open our souls at the same time. We must say: "Lord, tell us what a Christian should be. We don't ask anything more of you than that and we know that if *we* become fully Christian and *our brothers* become fully Christian we will become one in Christ, one in your Spirit." This is ecumenism at the grass roots. This is the building up of visible unity.

No one in the world reproaches us because we are Christian. I have never met anyone who said "I am reproaching you because you are Christian." What they *did* say is "I am reproaching you because you are not Christian *enough*." That is the reproach. If we can go ever more deeply into the movement of the Holy Spirit, if we can let him be revealed in each of us, well, I think the Holy Spirit through the Charismatic Renewal will bring the day of visible unity nearer and nearer to us. I don't think we should say, "Oh, be patient. It's the work of God." Of course, it is the work of God and we must in some way be patient. But you know, if you love someone, you are impatient to communicate that love. So we have to love that visible unity with all the impatience of God who wishes it, orders it and gives us that mandate. "Be one, like the Father is one in me, I in you and you in me." To our great surprise, we will see that the Go-Between working among the churches will not suppress the identity of all the different aspects, but will instead illuminate all the facets of the richness of Christ. He will just show us how to achieve unity out of diversity as the Holy Spirit does this in plurality. It is plurality in unity. This is the work of God. This is the action of God as a Go-Between on every level; on the family level, on the level of Christians, on the level of churches all together, and then, Go-Between between the Church and the world.

Archbishop Ramsey ended his talk by stressing that aspect. The Holy Spirit is at work in his people, but he is also at work everywhere in the world. Wherever the truth is spoken, it comes from the Spirit of God. Whenever a person is truly loving, it is really the Spirit loving in him. Whenever someone is making peace, he is the instrument of the Spirit of God. In all our contacts, in all our meetings, it is the promise of God that you will be blessed if you are the makers of peace.

We must listen to everything the Holy Spirit has to say to us. We have something to give but we also have something to receive and we must listen carefully in order to receive it. So much is asked

from us today in the work of social justice, in our
obligations to the third world, in all the problems of
daily life; and in all this the Holy Spirit has
something to say. Every morning when you open
your daily paper there is something there. The
Spirit of God is at work today just as he was in the
beginning, calming the waters. He is at work in the
chaos in society today. He even has something to
say to us in the present crisis of energy. Just look at
the fragility of our industrial civilization of which
we are so proud. Simply because of a shortage of
gasoline all of our lives are changed. The Holy
Spirit is asking us to accept the fullness of the
energy of the power of God and of the Church. We
lack that energy. So the Spirit is speaking to us
through all events, good or bad, great or small. We
must simply be open, open to the fullness of the
Spirit at work.

I hope that one day we will see Ecumenical unity
not only on the level of Christians living peacefully
together. Already we see a change on the level of
the theologians and you know it is much more
difficult to convert a theologian! At that level we
can see some progress; agreement about baptism,
agreement about the Eucharist and about ministry.
It is not a full agreement but it is a substantial one.
I hope that in a few years we will see agreement
about authority. Yesterday we heard Prior Schutz
speak so wonderfully about that idea of universal
unity. Existential unity, theological unity and I
surely hope one day soon, sacramental unity. It
was such a suffering for me yesterday. It was the
first time that, out of loyalty to the rules of today, I

could not participate in the Eucharist. I hope that those rules will be changed tomorrow but meanwhile we obey. It is just like when you are in city traffic and there is a red light, you must obey that red light in order to avoid disorder. However, one can question that red light and by discussion can get it changed to a green one. Well, I pray that one day the Spirit of God will bring us together there.

But to conclude, I would just like to share with you how very touched I was by a gesture on the part of one of your bishops. Just after Holy Communion, he knew what was in my heart, and it was in his heart too, and he just came to embrace me. I think this is a symbol. Let us do all that we can together in deep love and unity and the Lord will answer that prayer. He wants to answer this prayer more than any other prayer, because he told us to ask for the Spirit of God and it will be given to you, for your joy, for the joy of the Church, for the joy of God.

**The Most Reverend
John Maury Allin**

**Presiding Bishop of the
Protestant Episcopal Church**

God In Us

Oh God, by thy Holy Spirit, help me to allow thy Holy Spirit to speak through me. And oh God, help my brothers and sisters to hear. *Amen.*

As I came into this pulpit, I began that wrestling with the devil many of us encounter in the pulpit. As I looked forward to this moment, I was aware that usually what is expected is a learned homily, precise phrasing — previously delivered to the press, which I think takes the fun out of it — and I had to admit to myself that I cannot do that. To perform well, to be well-accepted, to be well-thought of — you see immediately the temptation and the distraction.

You are also under a temptation to listen to the
Presiding Bishop-elect — and not be attentive to
the Holy Spirit. I believe he can speak to us and
through me, even though I fail, stumble, stutter.
Your responsibility is to avoid becoming homiletical
judges, or looking for and being critical of
preaching techniques. Rather, all of us here should
seek to hear the message of God as he proclaims it
through the power of his Holy Spirit, as he reveals it
to us in the glorious life of our blessed Lord.

The first scriptural context in which I would like
to speak today is a verse from the fourth chapter of
the Gospel according to St. John: "God is Spirit,
and those who worship him must worship him in
spirit and truth." And then, from the fourth chapter
of the first Epistle of St. John: "God is love." The
twenty-third verse of the first chapter of St.
Matthew; the quotation from the Prophet Isaiah:
"Emmanuel: God is with us." And then, that
remarkable fourth chapter of the first Epistle of St.
John: "If we love one another, God is in us." And
lastly, our Lord's imperative in the nineteenth and
twentieth verses of the twenty-eighth chapter of St.
Matthew's Gospel: "Go, ye, into all the world,
proclaim this good news, the news that God is love.
Initiate, baptize all nations into this reality. Lo, I
am with you until the end of the ages."

From where we are, our own circumspection, our
own sensing, we perceive God. The clergy
remember seminary lectures on the mystery of the
Blessed Trinity which each class, in turn, undertook
to explain adequately. Indeed, I have heard
sermons on the Holy Trinity which were rather

convincing that God, after all, was a committee.

But meanwhile, you and I and all sorts of people, if we are in any way aware and open to life, sensitive, perceiving, can see God — God's spirit love, God creating in order to love, the glory of the universe, the remarkable wonder of each unique human life. We take it so for granted. We say, "Oh, I know Jesus well," when we don't really know ourselves. A great unexplored area that can fascinate us, for eternity, is our own inner workings. We take so much for granted. The glory of creation, knowing the power of a loving God at work, creating. We experience God in his redeeming power, understand him in human terms as revealed in Jesus Christ — loving, forgiving, reconciling, bringing back into relationship, uniting one with another. We experience his power in being loved, being forgiven, in spite of our inadequacies and failures. To admit them and still be loved is power divine, is love, is God.

And in spite of the distractions and problems of this world, its tensions, all of us are sustained by that experience of the renewing presence, the healing, the uplifting. Indeed, we can experience the presence and power of God, God's love, God the Spirit, even when our own experience is negative. When we see the dreadful effects of hate and prejudice, the destructive forces in the world, even in our most desperate moments, we realize a need for a God who could do something about our predicament. Indeed, we human beings experience over a whole scale, a whole spectrum, from the beatific vision to the lesser level of those moments when we tightly close our eyes and somehow try to tune in and reach up, as if he were out there somewhere, brooding over us.

Our human behavior regarding God is expressed in at least three ways. First of all, we replace him. We substitute. We substitute meanings for words. Love — what does it mean? We shuffle values. We create idols. Remember the golden calf? No man has seen God at any time, so we make our own provisions. To me, one of the most plaintive comments in all Scripture is Aaron's response to Moses, when he said, "We just put the gold in, and this calf came out." For them, God was up on that mountain, up in that power, in those clouds, in that lightning, and they had sent one brave man up to talk with him. In the meantime, they had become bored and they wanted a God, as you and I so frequently want a God that we can take along with us and put where we want to and use as we will. The calf — so symbolic — was economically meaningful. It suggested a power that they could commit themselves to and follow through the wilderness of their world.

We do the same thing. One does not have to point to what is happening in the world; one can look in the Church. We substitute system for the power of the living God. We even have the capability of substituting one old broken-down church, which we can make into a battleground. If one window is changed, it is as if you were changing the living God. There are people who have not been active for years who suddenly become activated in this new power and devotion to religion. I have often wondered whether Constantine did us a favor. He certainly put upon us from his day the burden of building churches — which we can use as symbols even substitutes for our God. We have to see God.

Our second behavior is reaction. And many times it is reaction out of fear, our desperate need to be secure, our desperate need for life. We clothe it in religious terms, but as our Lord said to the nobleman, "Except ye see signs and wonders, ye cannot believe." The fundamentalist accepts the Holy Bible as if it were an insurance contract. And God help you if you move one word. For the fundamentalist the words are the guarantee of that wonderful story he has not yet come to experience, and vainly hopes he will.

The classic temptations. Remember, after our Lord went down to John's baptism and washed himself in the contaminated water, taking the sins of all of us upon him, he was led out in the Spirit into the wilderness to experience, as we experience, those comprehensive temptations. First of all, think of the temptation in terms of our social concerns. If we suddenly discovered, by some means of manipulating God, that we did have the power to turn stones into bread, we could feed the world. And suppose the Episcopal Church alone gained the power — think what a marvelous thing that would be! I can see now, with that efficiency we have in General Convention, when that motion came up, someone standing and saying, "Mr. President, I move you, Sir, that we, by the will of this convention, make fourteen more tons of stone into bread and ship them off to the place where we've heard the plaintive cry."

The only problem is that you don't have to love anybody if you have more bread than you need.

And our Lord said that you do not live by bread alone. Bread is not the source of life. Love is the source of life. The power of the living God is among us, sustaining us in life.

I thought today, as I came to this place, what a marvelous thing it would have been if *The New York Times* could have announced this morning that at twelve noon the Presiding Bishop-elect of the Episcopal Church would jump off the tower of Riverside Church. I have more of a congregation than I deserve in the first place, but think of what we could have done to the traffic problems in the city. And further. Suppose I could have managed it. Think of the acute pride it would have produced — not just in me, I would have been impressed with myself — but the truth is you would have been infected with the same pride. You'd have said, "But one of our boys made it." And even more interesting, after three or four weeks (because if you can do that even once I think you could make it run for three or four weeks) — someone would say, "Are you going up to see that guy jump off the Riverside Church tower?" And someone would say, "No, I saw him do it once." So we dismiss God many times, and his power and his work. Many have looked at all creation and have not looked back. Except ye see signs and wonders.

And then that last, most subtle temptation of all, in which somehow we say, "If we can secure power in God's name, we can change the world." But we are never quite certain, it seems. At least we are always subject to distraction when we attempt to define power. Theocracy is, in the minds of many, one of the most destructive forms of government that was ever foisted on a people. We say it is under God's rule, but we must have a committee to administer the rule, and we will make the laws, and you will obey. We will decide what is good for you.

No. We must not be so tempted, for God does not so will. He loves, and walks with us through a life that, in itself, can be filled with wonder and awesomeness, a life in which we can find his glory and discover his love, within us and among us, around us and beneath us.

Have you ever thought of the significance of the little words — the prepositions? We so frequently become preoccupied with the big words. Indeed, we are not satisfied even with those. We invent new words.

But the key words are "in" and "among" and "between" and "around", "beneath" and "above."

The third behavior is to respond and obey. This can overcome the act of replacement, it can overcome the reaction and fear — in fact, it can cast out fear. "Follow me," said our Lord, "come and see where I live. Come live with me. I stand at the door and knock, and he that opens to me, I'll come in where he is, and I'll sup with him." Emmanuel; he is with us as we love one another. You and I are called, blessed. Make Eucharist in the reality that God allows us in obedience to share in the glory of creation, to build up, to offer ourselves. God allows us to experience redemption by sharing redemption. By accepting forgiveness and learning to forgive, God allows us to know the opportunity to come to the unique potential he has placed in each of us. We share in his love and his life in sharing it with one another.

He who says he loves God and hates his neighbor is a liar. That is a pretty straightforward statement. In these days and times you have to be careful, lest you launch forth from a text like that in the pulpit. Somebody will take it personally. But if we love one another, we are in God, in God's love, and he is in us, among us. And that glorious news, that wonderful experience is why Christ came and why, for our sakes, he would send us into all places — the uttermost parts of the earth — that we might share that love, initiate people into it.

And these days, brethren, while people are entitled to organize as they desire — the care that must be taken is that we do not let the new organizations, like the old organizations, frequently take the place of our God and our commitment to him. What I would suggest to you is that we of the clergy should take thought before we go further with all sorts of negotiating schemes and job descriptions. I am reminded of the young priest who said to the old bishop, "Well, Bishop, what do you want me to do in that mission?" And the bishop smiled at him and said, "I just want you to go and love them. By God's grace, maybe they'll come to know the love of God, and thereby know God."

The renewal of ministry must be an obedience that says, "Lord, where do you want me to be?" He may say, "Right where you are." "What do you want me to do?" "Love my sheep, love my children. Share that love with them, and I will be with you, and among you and in you and around you, and you will know my power and my glory."

We cannot do this alone. We may be physically separated from one another, but we must always realize it is only possible within the Lord, within the power of the Christ, within the body. All are not ears, all are not eyes, all are not hands, all are not feet, but together, incorporate, we share those functions. We support one another, correct one another, strengthen one another, renew one another in the love of God, the power of the Holy Spirit, beautifully, perfectly, gloriously reflected in Christ Jesus. Many of us came here with our fears, our anxieties, our distress, our ambitions, and our distractions.

Many of us came wondering what this exercise would be like. I do believe that if I began now to sing that contemporary Eucharistic hymn, "We are one in the Spirit, We are one in the Lord," all of us would sing with one voice in that oneness, that with-oneness that is communion, the community of the Holy Spirit. As the community of the Holy Spirit gathered, gathered in the love of God, we would sing, "We are one in the Spirit, we are one in the Lord."

Now to God the Father, God the Son and God the Holy Spirit be ascribed as his most justly due all might, majesty, dominion and power, both now and forever, world without end. *Amen.*

**The Right Reverend
Robert E. Terwilliger**

Suffragan Bishop of Dallas

Take Not Thy Holy Spirit From Me

A Sermon for Priests

"Take not thy Holy Spirit from me." Would he? Would God take his Holy Spirit from me? God is good. Would the Father withdraw the Spirit? Isn't this a negative way of thinking of God? Isn't this a terrible thing to pray, even though for centuries we have prayed it in the daily prayer of the Church. Have we prayed it without feeling, without fear? God would not do a thing like that.

We have very nice ways of thinking about the Holy Spirit, yet in the Scripture, the Holy Spirit is not nice. There are awful things said about the Holy Spirit in the Old and in the New Testaments. In the life of Jesus, he is born by the Spirit, he is baptized of the Spirit and, coming out of the waters of Baptism, the Spirit drives him into the wilderness to be tempted of the devil. Perhaps the most awful thing he ever said was about the Holy Spirit — that those who could not discern the Holy Spirit, those who saw his works and said they were the works of the devil, those who had turned darkness into light and light into darkness, had lost the forgiveness of God.

We are warned about the Spirit. We must not grieve the Spirit; we must not quench the Spirit. The Spirit in the New Testament is not to be taken for granted. He is the *Holy* Spirit; in the Spirit is the holiness of God, the awfulness of God's power and God's judgment. And he is not to be possessed! He is not to be taken for granted!

In the Fourth Gospel, the Holy Spirit is spoken of as wind. He comes and he goes. He goes as well as comes. He is uncontrollable as the wind is uncontrollable. And all this, of course, comes forth in the terrible story of Pentecost, where the Spirit comes upon the Church, consecrating it in wind and fire.

The Holy Spirit is dangerous. In fact, the whole realm of human spirit, and ghost spirit, and evil spirit — this is a realm of danger. Remember, some years ago, the lines in front of the theaters waiting to see *The Exorcist?* In 1973, when the conference was on *The Charismatic Christ,* Jesus was in. Then the devil was in. And this is not simply something casual. You do not wake up on a certain day, or in a certain year, or at a certain conference and say what, in the Gospel, is *in*. Though some people do, and attribute this to the Holy Spirit, which has a peculiar result at this moment — the Devil is in. This was a sign to us, as all the ins and outs are signs to us. It is a sign that we should read — man is made to be possessed, and if he is not possessed by the Spirit of God he will be possessed by evil spirits.

Perhaps that is what is meant by losing the Spirit — take not your Holy Spirit from me — because, if the Holy Spirit departs, it does not mean there is nothing, but that there is a terrible something. And the terrible something is the power of the demonic, the power beyond man. The realities that we are dealing with are not simply the realities of God and man, but the realities of God and man and evil power, and this we see now, and we find it believable, frighteningly believable.

Throughout this conference, I have been regaled with stories people have told you about devil possession, questions about exorcism. If you got on an airplane with your collar on, the stewardess came up to you and said that she had moments when she might be possessed by the devil. What kind of thing is this? How are we to regard it? A reporter chased the Archbishop Ramsey up into the tower of Riverside Church, where he was going to do a videotape, to have one minute with him on exorcism. Is this what we're talking about — "Take not thy Holy Spirit from me"? Yes, but yes and no, because the current obsession with devils is a manifestation of demonic power, for as we know perfectly well, the most appalling work of the devil is to persuade us that he is working somewhere else than where he is. All this business about exorcism is a demonic distraction from the works of the devil.

What are the works of the devil? The works of the devil are not things proceeding in dramatic, strange, weird, fascinating ways that capture the imagination and persuade you that you should subject yourself to two hours in a theater, be appalled and nauseated. The devil's works always masquerade as the works of God. "Take not thy Holy Spirit from us." Maybe it has been happening already. What is it? What is God doing? What is the evil doing in the world?

We have been involved in a tremendous out-pouring of fascination with the Holy Spirit; there have been strange signs. And we have been able to accept again some of the New Testament gifts of the Spirit that we thought were safely in abeyance. We have been experiencing things like *glossolalia* and prophecy. I suppose one of the reasons why many of you have been drawn here is that there is something being said — and that is, this phenomenon seems to be cooling now. Perhaps the charismatic movement has peaked. Is God withdrawing his Spirit? Not necessarily.

God has never promised to keep us in a state of feeling good. If you know the history of the Church, which is the history of the Spirit as well as the history of the human institution, you will know that, time and time again, special manifestations of God's power have been given, but they are not given forever to comfort and to console, to strengthen and to keep in a perfect state of assurance. Some of the most amazing and marvelous works of the Spirit are done in the dark night of the soul. The greatest work of the Spirit ever done was the work of the Spirit on the cross of Christ, when he took upon himself the predicament of man, even to the point of sharing, "My God, my God, why?" He was not in a state of consolation, he was in a state of dereliction and a state of resurrection by the Spirit. And even if these works of the Spirit should be withdrawn, that may still be a work of the Spirit calling us, as he calls us often in the pain and sometimes in the darkness of life. Indeed, this may well be the vocation of our communion at this moment. To remember, as we have sought to remind the Church before, that there is a tremendous covenant of normalcy and naturalness in the sacramental life, which is given to us by God's own deed in Christ. The works of the Spirit come and they go, but they are given also in signs and symbols, in holy moments, in appointments, if you will, that God makes with man through his covenant, his promise. These things we have been given. We have been baptized. We have been confirmed. We have been ordained. Perhaps we have been consecrated.. And if you have heard what the Spirit has been saying to the churches in this place, these acts are gifts of the Spirit. Given to be enlivened. Gifts of the Spirit — begun, not finished, begun in us to be renewed, ever renewed again and again in the Spirit.

However, they are not to be taken for granted. We are not to say we have the Spirit, we are baptized Christians, we are confirmed communi-

cants, we are validly ordained priests, we have the
Apostolic succession and we convey it by the
laying on of hands: We possess the Spirit. And those
who have this feeling, who act out this feeling,
reveal the terrible mystery of the withdrawal of the
Spirit. It is a strange thing and you can feel it sometimes in phenomena you see — hopefully, not
phenomena you cause. We have been seeing a great
many things that look like the absence of God. And
the absence of God, which shows itself sometimes
in the life of the priesthood, in the life of religious,
includes the things that we speak about so easily as
crises identity, vocation, and the rest — they can
have a terrible meaning. Sometimes we seem posi-
tively to think of them as a form of freedom, when
they are a form of lostness. And we cannot have
them forever.

I do not speak of individuals, and I do not speak
of all, but I do speak of something that is seen
sometimes more acutely by the laity than by the
clergy. That is, a man cannot go back upon the gift
that has been given to him in the Holy Spirit and
not have something happen to him. A religious
cannot forsake the vows without having something
happen, something that may not be immediately
apparent in the first fine, careless rapture of a new
life. But often, too often, and terribly, something
happens that becomes visible in the face, in the
word, in the life.

If we are truly called, we are called forever. If we
are truly ordained, we are ordained forever. And in
the power of the Spirit we must live, not taking the
Spirit for granted, but in a holy fear that, because

we do not respond to the Spirit, the gift of the Spirit may be turned into something terrible and relentless, in which, in some strange way, in the judgment of God, we cease to be.

This may seem a strange way to end a conference on the Holy Spirit. But I have not ended. "Take not Thy Holy Spirit from us" is a prayer that is always answered — if it is truly prayed. How is it prayed truly? By knowing to whom we pray. To the Father, who sends the Spirit. And knowing for what we pray — knowing who the Spirit is. And this may mean, time and again, remembering things we half forget in our excitement about the Spirit. There is one way in which we pray this prayer most truly. It is the way we pray it in the Book of Common Prayer at the beginning of the Eucharist, when we invoke the Spirit in a way the Archbishop mentioned this morning, as the one who convicts the world of sin. He convicts us of sin. He is the source of our penitence. "Almighty God, unto whom all hearts are open, all desires known, and from whom no secrets are hid, cleanse the thoughts of our hearts . . ." How? "By the inspiration of the Holy Spirit." When the Holy Spirit moves within us, he changes us by making us men and women of repentance, of change, of *metanoia,* of conversion. That means we have to accept the responsibility for the things we do and the things we are. And we must accept this responsibility in a Church that now seeks to avoid penitence and to denigrate sin and, therefore, is in danger of losing the Spirit.

There is no way to open yourself to the Spirit

without cleansing yourself, totally, completely, and utterly by the stirring of the Holy Spirit of God, who is the pure love of God. Therefore, in this moment, if you feel weak, if you feel shaken, if you feel unsure, if you would like to have more vocation apparent in your life, ask yourself this terrible question: "Must not something change within me? something be renounced? something confessed? something forgiven?" And will be forgiven, and it ever shall, and this is the perpetual way the Spirit is kept within life. When the Spirit comes, he convicts us of sin.

He does something else — he calls us. Vocation. Vocation means being open to the call. Vocation is not something we had, or something we have. It is something that has us. We respond to vocation. We listen. For receiving the Spirit and not losing the Spirit means listening to the Spirit, being open to the Spirit. The Church must be an open Spirit, be an open Church.

What does this mean — to be an open Church? Does it mean that we, therefore, say anything is possible within the Church? Anything can happen within the Church. Isn't this exciting! The Church may become something it never was before. No. Because whenever the Spirit moves, and whenever we are open to the Spirit, what is formed is Christ, and obedience to Christ. Receiving the Holy Spirit is another way of saying "Yes" to Christ. An open Church is an obedient Church, and this leads directly into that tremendous thing the Archbishop said this morning: "The Veni Creator and the crucifix belong together." "Come, Holy Spirit," "Not my will, but yours be done." "Father, forgive them." "Into Thy hands I commend my Spirit." "It is finished."

The consummation that comes in vocation comes in the cross and the resurrection, and nowhere else. It does not mean some kind of fulfillment, which is, somehow, an ultimate manifestation of my essential ego. It means not I, but Christ. And it means saying, "Yes," in this fashion, and not necessarily in some beautiful, great, clear-cut moment of decision. It means going back to where you are, to where you are put, to whatever the address of your Calvary may be. This is the place of vocation. It means dealing with your vestry, with the neurotic on the telephone, with your bishop, with your prayers, with the tiredness and the weakness and the difficult decision, and with the dangerous speaking of the word of God, and the presence of your body where the place of witness to justice must be. It means study. It means faithfulness in your family and to your wife. It means the preparedness for sacrament. And it means aging in the service of Christ and not being bitter — you know what it means. It may mean the thing you came here to get away from.

Vocation is something that keeps going on, and on, and on. It is another way of saying, "Deny yourself, take up your cross, and follow me." Through life, through death, to life again. Because the one who calls us by his Spirit, and to the Spirit, is the one who waits, the one who is waited for, the one who is beyond life and beyond the world, at the end of it all. At the world's end. At our end. We are being moved toward him. Feel that movement

— it has happened here among us. We are being moved. Not simply stirred, but moved, and moved toward him. We have been gathered up for a moment, and we sense that we are on the pilgrimage that goes from here to there, to a place unknown — no, to someone whom we know, who waits, and calls, and stirs. To the one who has empowered us through our journey, who has given us the Spirit that was given to him, and, therefore, in the power of that Spirit, we shall move. And move the Church, and in that movement, we shall go where he goes until, strangely, we reach him.

Take not your Holy Spirit from us, Lord, because without the power of your Spirit, we shall be lost. Take not your Holy Spirit from us, Lord, but give to us your Holy Spirit, that things may happen through us and in us that we cannot do. Come, Holy Spirit, come.